Rise and Fall

Rise and Fall

A Memoir of Drug Abuse

Sheila Prior

iUniverse LLC
Bloomington

RISE AND FALL
A Memoir of Drug Abuse

iUniverse books may be ordered through booksellers or by contacting:

iUniverse LLC
1663 Liberty Drive
Bloomington, IN 47403
www.iuniverse.com
1-800-Authors (1-800-288-4677)

ISBN: 978-1-4917-3741-5 (sc)
ISBN: 978-1-4917-3743-9 (hc)
ISBN: 978-1-4917-3742-2 (e)

Library of Congress Control Number: 2014910680

Printed in the United States of America.

iUniverse rev. date: 06/10/2014

This is the personal story of a young man's journey, from experimenting with pot at age fourteen to developing a deadly heroin addiction by age thirty. Through his mother's search for an understanding of this destructive path, this book was born.

Preface

My husband and I retired at sixty-two and fifty-five years of age, respectively. We owned our home, a vacation home, and a time-share at the beach. We had raised three kids and had traveled extensively over the years with and without our children. After our two girls and our son were married and starting their own families, my husband and I began to complete our bucket list and were having the time of our lives.

Then it happened.

Our son nearly died from a heroin overdose. Our entire family was clueless that he'd even been suffering from an addiction. Years earlier, my father died, and at that time, I was sure I could never experience such deep pain again. Much to my dismay, this gut-wrenching experience was no less painful, though it was a different kind of pain. I knew how to grieve and deal with death. I had no knowledge of how to deal with drug addiction and with an addict. My first instinct as a mother was to control and fix the situation. This was my first mistake.

We were actually on a two-week tour from New Mexico to Wyoming when we got the news. Halfway through the trip, the park rangers found us and informed us to call home. My husband's mother had died, and we were unable to get home in time for the funeral. Also we learned our son had been arrested for residential burglary to support the drug addiction, about which we were clueless.

Once we finally did get home, the reality of it all hit us extremely hard. I cried a lot and finally called my doctor for a sleep aid. I was tired and emotionally drained. The death of my husband's mother had not been totally unexpected, but it was still emotional. Coupling that with our fair-haired son, a family man and successful paramedic who owned ten rental properties and his own home, landing in prison, it was more than a little hard to swallow.

People are very different in how they deal with disaster. I am much stronger than I ever imagined. My biggest problem was the lack of knowledge I had about how to help a drug addict. My husband had a more difficult time and started seeing a therapist to learn to cope and function again. Our blissfully happy life and wonderful family had gone to hell in a handbasket overnight—or so it seemed. Our girls were angry with our son because of the way his addiction was affecting everybody they loved. Finally, we all got in the car and found an Al-Anon meeting at a church that had a babysitting service. We put our son's daughter in the day care and sat through an enlightening experience.

On the way home, we realized that this was not our fault and we had no control over it. We also realized that, as bad as we thought our problems were, they actually paled in comparison to what we had just heard in that Al-Anon meeting. Somehow the realization of what was happening to us was not unique, and it helped us to see that people of all walks of life deal with—and survive—drug addiction every day. It is beneficial to hear other people say they love their children, but they do not enable them with money or try to intervene when their loved ones hit rock bottom in a jail cell—because the alternative all too often is death.

It was the hardest thing I have done in my life, but I left my son in that jail for many months without even going to visit him. I was afraid that if I saw his face, I would spend every dime I had to get him out of jail. Finally after many meetings and therapy, I decided it was time to write him a letter and tell him how I felt. He wrote me back and began to explain his entire secret life that he'd led right under our noses. I have decided to share that with the world. Somehow it makes me feel better, and it might give some other mother a clue that I missed.

Introduction

Once my son finally revealed his double life to me in letters from jail, I felt the need to share my thoughts and experiences with other people. I wasn't really shocked about a little pot in high school. I was not naive to teenagers using fake IDs, sneaking into nightclubs, and smoking a little pot. Most of us have done those things and then have been in church the following Sunday morning to keep parents uninformed and off our backs—small price to pay for running with the cool kids. I suppose, in some respects, I had lived the same way, making people happy by saying what they wanted to hear. I should not have been surprised or shocked to learn my son did the same thing to me, just on a much higher level. The difference has basis in scientific fact; his mind and body would not allow him to stop and walk away when the party was over. He pushed the envelope to the brink of death. We hear about famous stars doing this all the time. They die young.

I will attempt to elaborate on our feelings as a family and as a mom at the end of each chapter. This will be a reflection of what I have now learned was happening then—that being during the past fifteen years. We've heard all our lives that *ignorance is bliss.* It is absolutely true. Apparently we prefer *ignorance is bliss* to *ignorance is no excuse.*

Regardless of the fault or the blame or the guilt, this story, my son's story, is happening every day to people of all walks of life, right under our noses. This is how our situation unfolded, as told to me by my son in letters from jail.

If I am honest, I am more than a little embarrassed to start this account of my life. To say that I have lead a double life would be something of an understatement. From the beginning, I have always had what I needed in life. My parents have always been good providers and overly sufficient role models, always giving me plenty of money and emotional support. I have never been out of a job or had trouble making friends. So now you may ask how a person with a lot of support and seemingly good instincts ended up in county lockup, awaiting sentencing and transport to prison. The answer still eludes me as I sit in this cell thinking about that very question. I can, however, explain from my viewpoint what your child may be thinking or even doing while you're showering them with all the support you're sure you should.

Complicated as this may all be, the first thing you should know is some children, yes, even yours, may be born with different brain chemistry. Some people's brains process drugs and alcohol differently than others. All that being said, this is my story from around the time I started my experimentation with drugs and alcohol, at the age of fourteen, to where I am today, at the age of thirty. Please use this book as a guide to understand the balance your children will strike between school, sports, girlfriends, and drug use. Look for examples and similarities in your life and theirs to my story. If you do this, you can begin to understand what you can do to first recognize drug use and then combat it on your own terms.

Our family

One

My family consists of my two parents, my father (an administrator at work and at home), sets down rules and gives praise when warranted, and my mother, an immunologist and union representative, much like a cheerleader with a firm bottom line. I have one older sister, who has always been around for her little brother and very successful in her work life. Finally my last and younger sister could pass for my twin. She is full of love and not afraid to show emotion. If I am honest, she is the most successful in her work life. This introduction to my family is very short and lacking in information. I will elaborate more as it applies to the story. It should be enough to get us started.

Brother and sister

The year I went from middle school to high school, I was fourteen years old. I had two friends that lived close to me. One of the two got some pot, and I had my first experience with illegal drugs. I remember feeling very nervous, but more so excited about the thought of trying this substance I thought was so cool from movies and TV shows from my generation. We smoked the stuff in my father's garage that was attached to the house through the door the whole family uses to go in and out of the house. Both of my friends left soon after.

The pot does something funny to a new user. It immediately makes you paranoid; thinking that Mom, Dad, or even the police will know what you have done. This feeling lessens as you build a tolerance to the drug. So my first experience was like an adventure—changing my shirt, throwing away the one I was wearing to hide the smell. I washed my face at least three times. About this time my mother and father pulled up together in the very garage we had been smoking in earlier. My father immediately smelled the weed and walked up to me and said, "You better never smoke that stuff at my house again." With that, he let the issue pass.

I was happy about that due to the fact that I was reeling from my first joint ever. From there I was off to the races, as they say. At the end of each school day, instead of our normal bike riding and fishing, my friends and I would be smoking. First we had enough weed and time to smoke the weed before our parents returned home from work. This was the first change in my life for the sake of drugs. I don't think that this particular change in my life was so significant, being that I forsook riding my bike and roller skating for hiding in the woods and smoking very small joints. But it's the behavior of accepting the drug as fun or adventurous, and then—this is the worst part—successfully hiding the drug. I don't mean hiding it in my room or in the bushes; what I mean is much more dangerous. And what I believe is the biggest problem for me and will be your biggest problem, is spotting drug use in your child or loved one—especially if your child is personable or well spoken. No, the hiding that I speak of is the ability to consume the drug and maintain life as if nothing is going on. This is my biggest problem, I believe. Given, at the age of fourteen, there are not many responsibilities to maintain.

But as you will see, as the story and my drug life progresses, maintaining a good outward appearance and well-mannered behavior will hide drug use for many years before it catches up to the user. Problem is, by then, the user may be sitting in a jail cell or worse.

The summer seemed to go very quickly. All I did was pretend to go fishing or riding bikes on the trail. Next on my young agenda was high school, nervous as I was about girls and bigger bullies. When a child leaves middle school, he or she is the biggest dog on the block. But on that the first day of high school, I was in another world. There were so many different types of people. Of course my buddies from middle school were there. As luck had it, one of them even was old enough to drive now, as he was kept back a grade at a younger age.

Looking back, I must have looked nervous walking through the high school hallways as a freshman. Sports are what made me feel like a part of my high school; I had always been athletically inclined. Baseball and soccer filled my youth every season at County Recreation Ball. When soccer season started, I met some new friends on my team. For some reason I gravitated to friends with similar interests, such as pot and my newfound adventure—Adderall pills—that one of my childhood friends was prescribed. Snorting these pills was all the rage when I was in high school. They gave me the feeling of being super alert, or having lots of energy with the ability to concentrate.

My friend who was able to drive, of course, drove me to and from school on the days I did not have soccer practice. This allowed me, for the first time in my life, to meet up with friends whose houses I could not walk to. We would meet at the local lake, where we would smoke pot and have the occasional beer instead of going to class. I would keep my skipping school to days that I did not have soccer practice. I was able to cover up the smell and use eye drops to keep my eyes from being red. I have always been good at talking to anybody about mostly anything. Making people laugh and being respectful of others has always afforded me the ability to fly under the radar.

As my freshman year ended, I got to be rather good at using pot and Adderall pills, all the while keeping my grades in check and my attendance under the radar. As you will see in chapter two, in the beginning of my sophomore year in high school, this began to change.

Slowly, these will be warning signs in your children that something is amiss.

You have to understand that, seeing me day to day, I had a smile on my face. I dressed very nicely, ran with the popular kids in my class, and always had at least a passable girlfriend.

This is going to be the problem—when I am in your face, you will be convinced everything is fine. What you have to look at is the pattern of grades and attendance with your child in school.

Our son was one of the best-dressed kids in school. We all found him to be a little over the top with his clothes. He was always ironing his pants, which was part of his disguise. He was also a standup comedian. The only problem we saw was that he loved hanging out with his friends and hated schoolwork. I attributed that behavior to the difference between girls and boys. At this time I did not see warning signs or bizarre behavior. His friends all seemed to have decent parents and home lives. I thought I was a good judge of character. If your kids dress nicely and have a good home life, you must be okay people. *I thought the kids that looked like hoodlums must be hoodlums. As it turned out, I was worried about the wrong crowd. Never judge a book by its cover.*

Two

As I waited for my second year of high school to begin, I was excited and less nervous than my freshman year. It seemed like I had everything to look forward to and nothing to fear. I seemed like no matter what extracurricular activities I got myself involved in (i.e., drugs), I was able to maintain good grades and attendance. Looking back, the passable attendance was due to the fact that I was unable to drive to school until my junior year. This did not stop me from occasionally skipping school to partake in volleyball at the lake or just go back to my house as both my parents would be at work.

My sophomore year was the first time I started to see negative effects from drug use in my life. Looking back it would be all too obvious to spot something that was amiss. The most obvious effect was my attendance dropped, but not so much that it set off any alarms. But I got more comfortable missing a day here and there with no negative effects. Greed set in. My father noticed that my perfect attendance fell to one or two days a week of missing in action. With this, grades will eventually drop off. Not that the effects of some pot and the occasional Adderall pill made me dumber, but missing a day a week caused me to miss test days or the review day for the test. My teachers began to have concerns and contacted my parents.

The jig was up, as they say. Being a very personable young man, I told my parents that one of my new friends and I were going to the lake and playing volleyball. You know, physical activity, bonding, new high school type stuff, most of which was true or at least felt true. The rest, I just left out about the drug use and the drinking. One day that stuck out in my mind the most was when I set out for school with a friend, and we literally rode through the parking lot, just giving my parents enough time to get to work. Before the first period bell rang, my teacher had a note to contact my dad to alert him to my absence. He wasn't at work yet, and I was already back at home smoking a joint. I had made myself a bowl of cereal and left the box out on the counter.

I was upstairs in my bedroom when I heard the distinctive three beeps of our home alarm. I knew right away I was busted. I knew in my mind that dealing with this now would not be in my best interests, as I was reeling from my early morning joint. I quickly hid under my bed. I heard my dad's disapproving tone as he made his way up our staircase. He must have yelled for me to come out for ten minutes. I lay still, like we were playing hide-and-seek, like we used to in the yard at night. Much to my surprise, he left, most likely because he had never made it to work and was already late. It was a small victory that only lasted until he got home from work that evening and promptly grounded me from riding to school with friends.

I'm still not sure why I thought I could skip school that day and have nobody notice. I just was not giving my normal amount of thought to cover myself. My thoughts were on making sure I had enough pot to smoke and the more difficult task of seeking a private location to first partake and then to cover up the smell, the red eyes, and the nervous behavior. Still, I managed to maintain a B average and keep myself out of any major attendance problems. From the outside looking in, I was always well dressed, wore a big smile, was easy to talk to, kept my wits about me, and had an easygoing attitude. This easily masked otherwise obvious changes in my behavior.

I mean, the evidence was there, but when you live with someone day to day who is taking steps to assure you with his or her outward appearance and personality, it becomes harder to see. Day to day, nothing is being thrown in your face that something is wrong. Instead, you see the overall big picture. For example, "absences" that are not there before or grades that are lower than usual. However, as a sophomore, my grades were still descent, and I still played school sports. Couple that with the fact that I did not yet have a driver's license, and nothing really jumped out enough to set off any alarms. This would soon change once I acquired every child's dream—a driver's license.

My husband is more strict, more sensible than I am; he spent some time in the military so ... these "rules" that he wants everybody to live by did not exactly work out for our son's then new truancy issues. Smoking a little pot with the kids at school might have been more acceptable than missing a day of education. However, who hasn't skipped school now and then? I did it.

My husband and I did all the things parents do when a child skips school. We made him ride the bus and restricted his favorite activities and threatened not to let him drive when he got his license. We had dealt with a similar situation with our oldest daughter, and the restrictions worked on her. Our son seemed appropriately humbled by the punishments. However, I must confess after a few days of it, he charmed me into letting him off. I doubt my weakness had little to do with eventual heroin use. I do wonder if I should have practiced tougher love, even for minor infractions.

Three

The ultimate freedom! The driver's license! My birthday fell at the beginning of summer, putting me younger than my classmates. As my sophomore year ended, my dad got me a Ford Bronco II. That summer, I got my first job at BI-LO grocery. I bagged groceries and cleaned the bathrooms at the end of the day. I made employee of the month my first month on the job. I was fired the next month for stealing a large bag of candy. I know that is not the most flattering note, but that is certainly not the most embarrassing part of my life I will share.

With my well-groomed looks and versed vocabulary, I walked across the street and got a job the same day at a pizza store. My manager was a very attractive girl. I decided right away that we should be more than friends. By the third week, I found that I had a unique skill. I could throw pizza in the air like the New York style pizza shops. Anyway, one night, we were the last two people in the shop, and I was helping her close the store. I was cleaning the topping line, and she was standing behind me cleaning the oven. Our backs touched and we did not pull away. We stood there for a moment.

I am telling you this because I was on cloud nine—nervous but excited. Only my new ride and drugs gave me anything close to this feeling. After that, I clocked out and politely said good-bye and left. On the way home, I thought about how to handle this situation. I called and asked if she was okay because she was the last one there for the night. That was it. The next day, I called and asked her to come over and help me study some math problems to help me prepare for next year's classes.

My parents have always been very supportive of my sisters and me. My mother takes our happiness just as seriously as our success. She is of the opinion that what's the point if you are miserable. My parents thought that an older girlfriend taking my time was still better than me running the streets with my new high school friends. It seemed like all I got from those friends were habits my parents did not approve of. Before the summer was over, my new girlfriend had moved in with my family.

As the next school year started, I finally had my own ride. I went to school early each day to show off my new ride. As soon as that wore off, I was back to skipping school with my friends. Soccer tryouts were during the second semester. I made the first practice and noticed we had a new coach; he was my old middle school coach. I knew I was a sure thing for the season. At the beginning of the second practice, he pulled me to the side and told me that I was unable to play due to me missing too many days of school.

To me, this was the first serious impact of my drug use. I mean, this one hurt. I immediately started looking for that feel-good feeling that I got from my girlfriend, but she was back in school for something or other at the time, so I decided to use my newfound freedom to get high with my friends. I got comfortable with my truancy issues, and before the end of the school year, I was suspended indefinitely. I was given the opportunity to attend a school for those who cannot follow the rules. The school was an alternative school. This is where I had the opportunity to meet all the other kids who seemed to have similar interests in drugs. Thanks for that!

This was where I was introduced to ecstasy. My girlfriend liked to dance, and my being well under twenty-one left us with few choices for late-night dance spots. At this time, raves became popular in town. A new friend and I hung out a lot, and this is where I would spend evenings when my girlfriend was in school. My girl had another friend she would spend time with. One night we all went out to a rave party at the abandoned local mall. The two of them hit it off instantly and we were set. Her friend and my friend began to date.

We went to the rave parties every other weekend—even one as far as two states away. Our drug of choice at this moment was ecstasy. The effect of this drug is an overall feeling of euphoria. It raises your body temp and makes you see things that are not really there and keeps you awake all night. This would leave me very tired and half-asleep for classes on Monday. This, combined with the weekly trip to the lake instead of school, would leave my grades worse than ever. So, to sum up my senior year, I had a really sweet girlfriend, a new car to drive to school, a new drug to add to my arsenal, the worst grades and attendance record ever, and I was attending alternative school. The only thing I felt the need to keep up was my appearance. If you were to speak to me, you would never suspect anything was going wrong. My parents always made sure I was well provided for, so I never felt the effects of my behavior.

Well as all parents do, we truly did dread our son getting a driver's license, mainly because we feared he would never go to school. I knew how much he hated school, so when the board of education informed us that he was going to be put in an alternative school for his truancy issues, I was relieved. I figured the only way to keep him in school was with a locked fence. I had given up on the idea of college for him. My new goal was a high school diploma.

He had a serious girlfriend who was smart and helped him with his schoolwork. We were a little surprised to find out much later that she was older than our son. She was so petite, adorable, and looked so young. After the entire family had fallen in love with her, we found out she was actually twenty-one years old. Eventually, given her situation, she more or less moved into our home, almost as one of the sisters. Our son's truancy and grade issues improved, so we were back on track.

It never occurred to me that I had allowed the board of education to put my son in an environment full of drug addicts.

I should have figured that was the case, but I chose to believe they were just kids who would rather play video games and skip school. Later I learned they were drug addicts—violent kids as well as truants. We had surrounded him with the kids we hoped to avoid. But it did allow him to improve his grades and graduate from high school, and at the time, that was a major goal and accomplishment.

Four

Talk about excited. When you're going into your senior year in high school, you feel as if you are on top of the world. You know you're going to be the oldest in the school. Gone are the worries of older classmates always seeming cooler than you. You yourself get to see what it's like to be looked up to for a change.

I was still with my girlfriend. She was still in school in the evenings and working at her mother's business. In my town, most likely just like yours, families own and operate their own businesses. I actually started working there in the summer before my senior year and after school when the school year started. It was not the most manly of jobs, but I was paid well and got to spend more time with my girlfriend. I was all for it.

The rave scene was still a small part of my life. My friend and I began to experiment with cocaine, and as we hung out more, I was always able to move from one drug to another without getting hung up on one drug in particular. As I look back, this is the reason I have made it as far in my life as I have. Moving from one drug to another gives you time to heal in one department while another suffers. For example, pot would make me slow and lazy, while cocaine would make me fast and overly productive.

So that was my drug life; my actual life was moving on with my senior year. My grades were always right on the line. To be honest, I was so taken with my older and very pretty girlfriend, good money at work, and my own ride that I really don't remember the particulars of my senior year. The highlights were that I went just enough not to get in more trouble. My grades seemed to walk the line between B's and C's on average. Keep in mind that was with as little effort as possible. I guess, in my head, I was already done with school, as I thought my personal life was as good as it possibly could be.

Much to my parents delight, I did graduate high school and walk to receive my diploma. The summer I graduated from high school, I moved out of my parents' house. In fact, the weekend I graduated, I moved into one of my dad's rental properties. Dad had a substantial amount of real estate that he'd purchased and rented to supplement his retirement. So my girlfriend and I lived about eight miles from where I grew up. It was only a two-bedroom, one-bath house, and looking back, it was a huge downgrade from how I was used to living, but the fact that it was mine made it the hottest house on the block. This was the first time in my memory that drugs played such a large part in my life.

What I mean is this was the first time in my life that I was spending the majority of my money on drugs and had to hide it from more than just my parents.

Cocaine was the drug. The summer I graduated, I was spending almost everything I made at work buying and snorting cocaine. I found that I enjoyed speed more than past drugs I had done because it gave me the ability to do more in one day than I could have done without it. I could stay up all night, party with friends, and go to work the next day with no problem.

Then, something happened to me that was new. I realized that I had a problem and I was unable or unwilling to do anything about it. I remember one night, when I was up all night, driving back and forth to my dealer's house, begging him to give me just a little more coke. I was broke and upset. Sitting on the couch at my new home with my fiancée asleep in bed, I got myself together enough to take a personal stand. I decided I was going to be done feeling like less than a man.

While sitting on my couch, crying like a baby, I wrote a note to my girl, who had no idea about the coke. You have to understand I was an expert by now at covering up my drug life. I was well groomed, funny, easygoing, and people loved me. Nobody had any idea what I was doing, not even people who lived in the same house with me. So I was pouring my heart out to my girl, telling her how I was spending all my money on cocaine and how I was feeling like less of a man. I remember I could not wait until morning to give it to her.

When she was reading it, her face told me her innermost thoughts. Halfway through the letter, she started crying. We went to bed and she held me all night.

I felt two hundred pounds lighter having gotten this off my chest. I thought once I shared this information with somebody that it would somehow make it easier for me to abstain. I had come full circle, and it did actually work. I stopped using cocaine and went back to smoking weed. This was a more relaxing high. I seemed to be able to maintain and only use weed occasionally. The cocaine had been every day and all day. The pot seemed to bring some paranoid behavior on, so I only did that at home watching movies.

With the support of my fiancée and a renewed since of manhood, I began to do things again besides running back and forth to the dope man's house. I started physical activity again. I ran into the dad of one of my high school friend at a gas station. He worked at our local ambulance service. It hit me like a ton of bricks. That is what I would do.

I got busy checking out what it took to become an EMT and then a paramedic. It helped that my father, whom I'd always respected, and in private have always wanted to obtain half of the professional status he has, was also an EMT around the same age as me. So I found that our local technical school had a certificate program that took eight months to complete. I signed up right away. My fiancée could not have been more proud of me. My family, especially my father, was happy and hopeful that the problems in my life were maybe changing.

When the EMT class started, I met a different set of friends. My girl and I were having no problems. I was about done working at the nail salon; my manhood got the best of me. That and a few of my "old friends" worked at a local store making deliveries, and they told me the store was hiring. The plan was to work there while I attended EMT school. As you will soon see, it is not always good to take up with old friends who have bad habits.

Looking back on my son's rave days, I had seen raves on TV, but that was all the knowledge I had. I loved to dance and I loved nightclubs, so I figured he liked to dance too. I knew his girlfriend did because we would all dress up and go to Halloween parties and dance.

I knew my children were social drinkers, and I did not feel uncomfortable about it. Raising the drinking age to twenty-one was not going to keep it from them, as we all know. I allowed them to drink at the pool at home, which dispelled the mystery of drinking, and they were always responsible.

None of them got in trouble with underage drinking. I was relieved when my youngest turned twenty-one. I am not ashamed to say our family parties together and does so responsibly. When they were old enough, we would rent a limo and go to Halloween parties or concerts so no one needed to drive. It was social and never excessive. After all, the family that plays together, stays together—or so I thought.

I had absolutely no idea my son was snorting cocaine. My husband has some allergies, and I remember from time to time thinking my son looked red-eyed and that his nose was running. I would leap into mother mode and start giving him allergy medications. I saw absolutely no signs of drug abuse. If his girlfriend had known, I think she would have told his sisters or me. Nobody saw it then.

I do remember eye drops everywhere, in the car, in his room, and in the bathroom. I remembered when I used to sneak around in high school; everyone had eye drops. Again I did think about pot but it never really stuck because of his prep school image and behavior. Because he was talking about going to EMT school, we thought this girlfriend was really working out. At all other times, he hated school; it was such a great surprise to hear him talk about going to school voluntarily. I got over my negative thoughts.

Five

At that point in my life—I'm going to be honest—I felt like everything was going well. My parents had been investing in rental property since I was ten or eleven years old. My father used to take me to his properties and have me help clean, paint, and watch his back, as some of the properties were not in the best parts of town. I was in my own place, in Grovetown, with my fiancée. The house was one of my father's rentals, and he gave me a break on the price. I had just finished my EMT course at Tech and seemed to have left my recent cocaine problem in the past. Everything was going really well. I was sticking with my occasional joint and a few beers in the evening.

I did very well in EMT school. Looking back, it was probably thanks to a combination of lessened drug use and being genuinely excited about the field I was trying to enter. I also had a very personal instructor, female, which for me is always key. I'm not saying I flirted my way through or anything, but I have always been able to come to terms with most any female if I so choose. As school went along, I continued to work at the store making deliveries.

My drug use leveled off until a former classmate from my high school days started to work there as well. We began to work on the same truck together. It seemed like every day we would push our casual drug use a little further. I remember when he and I would begin drinking a couple of beers at eight thirty in the morning on the way to our first delivery. This was followed by a few Janes after our first delivery. The drug testing policy was relaxed at best, so this was no problem. I guess I always thought I was about to stop my drug use altogether when I finished school, or after I got married, or soon as this or that. Needless to say, that never actually happened.

It seemed like school went rather quickly. I passed with flying colors. Something like an A–B average. As soon as the written portion of my EMT course was finished, I began the hands-on portion. This consisted of several hours of practicals in different areas. First and most obvious was riding on in an ambulance. Then came hours of working in the local area Emergency Department, followed by fewer and fewer hours in more specialized areas, such as the burn center, etc.

I was fully involved in what I was doing. The more exposure I got, the more I understood. I had found what I was good at, something that made me happy—made me feel like I had found what I was going to do. I was going to be following in my father's footsteps. He had worked EMS at a similar stage in his life. I was also being groomed to start my own rental property management, like my father.

After EMT school was over, I was only twenty years old. To work on an ambulance in the state of Georgia, for insurance reasons, you need to be twenty-one. My fiancée, who had also recently finished her degree in business, started a new job away from her mother's business—a company you would surely to be familiar with. She became a customer service representative.

After what seemed like forever, I finally turned twenty-one. I got hired on our local ambulance service. That was it; I started immediately. We had a contract with the VA hospital and also did most of the nonemergency transports around and out of town.

I was still nervously smoking pot, and at that point, I had figured out that I had a small taste for opiates. The particular form was mostly pain pills. It was my first experience with them. That was soon after my fiancée had some sort of "female" procedure, and I tried a few of hers.

We decided that it was time to get married, as we had been together since my sophomore year of high school. We had dated and lived together for about six years before I popped the question. We got married the following year. I was newly twenty-two years old, working at a job that I fully enjoyed, and my parents were talking about helping us move out of my father's rental and into a house of our own. Everything was like a fairy tale; I should have been satisfied with that.

There was always something inside of me that wanted to do something different. Not really sure what, but I never felt fully fulfilled unless I could smoke a joint, drink a beer, or do something at the end of the day. I had always had a feeling that I was working for a reward like that. Like, if I could not do that, what was the point of doing everything else? That is a selfish sounding feeling. How could someone who seemingly had everything still not be satisfied? I think that was a major part of my ultimate downfall. From where I sit today, I wish I could have half of that back; the job, the house, hell, even the simple amount of freedom to work outside seems like more than enough to me. It's funny how simple things can seem like so much when you're sitting where I am today.

So there we were. We had finally set a date to marry; I was finished with EMT school and had started a new job; I was in the process of purchasing a new home and several rental properties. All the while I still had a hidden drug habit that, at this point in my life, consisted of weed, pain pills, and what was starting to become a heavy drinking habit.

As parents, we were relieved our son was showing an interest in his future, making good grades, and helping his dad paint and fix up rental properties.

This girl had seemingly turned his life around, something we had not been able to do. We loved her and were excited about them getting married. Our son was suddenly aspiring to be like his father. We were not rich, but we made good investments, took the kids on great vacations, and everybody had a decent car and enough money for whatever they really needed.

Our son and his sisters were always very close. His sisters loved his fiancée and we loved family gatherings. We would all go to Braves games in a limo or to a concert if a band we liked was playing somewhere. We were a happy family and enjoyed each other's company. We enjoyed summers at the lake, boating, and hosting birthday pool parties at the house.

All this time, I never noticed my son acting differently. He never got drunk and always had a quick wit, and we all laughed at him being his comedic self. Now looking back on those cherished years, I do wonder if he used comedy as a mask. If so, I did not recognize it because he had been a comedian since he was two years old. And his daughter takes after him in this regard.

As parents we feel guilty about what our son has robbed our beautiful granddaughter of. She is the one who makes us laugh, and she is so much like him. The pain we feel over how much she misses having her dad present is indescribable.

Six

Soon after I started at the ambulance service, my fiancée and I moved into my first purchased home. I was very excited and was sure things in my life were going the way they should. I know now it was not, but it seemed like the day after we moved, we began to plan our wedding. She and I were married outside at a convention center. The wedding was huge. It seemed to me like I knew only a few people there; I remember my ambulance partner at the time came with his wife. The wedding was beautiful; my family was happy, I felt very proud of my life and the decisions I was making.

It's funny how things in your life open different opportunities for you. Since I now had my own place, I spent a lot of time during the day at home. I was working the twenty-four hour shift at work. This meant I would work twenty-four hours on and then have forty-eight off. The money I was making was more than enough with my wife also working at the time to pay all our bills and be able to afford most any reasonable luxury.

With all the time to myself during the day, I started to hang with some old friends a little more than before. The previous eight months had been pretty much consumed by school, wedding plans, and moving to the new house. I had a friend who had an idea to make some extra money. Since my place was empty two or three days with just me there till my wife made it home from work, we began to keep the stuff at my house. This, I thought to myself, was done for access for myself. So there I went, and I finally got to have my drugs without the cost.

My relationships at work were all good, my family life was good, and there were seemingly no adverse effects of my habitual drug use. I was managing my habits. As I was new with the ambulance service, I was careful with just how many drugs I would use. I got a feel for just how often they administered drug tests and more importantly how to tell when they were about to administer the tests. I was not on drugs at the time they would have adverse effects on me if I altogether stopped or cut back. What I mean by that is occasional use of pain pills will not have you going through withdrawal symptoms if you stop. Using pot will not ever give you withdrawal symptoms. The drinking, which was my biggest vice, will. I would begin to fill grumpy after thirty-six hours. I would not notice any problems during my twenty-four hour shift, but by the next night, if I had not had a drink, I would begin to have some upset stomach and attitude problems.

When I was at work I kept myself from crossing the line. I was, at the time, convinced I would not be using any drugs or drinking. This did not last. My immediate boss was another of many important female figures in my life. It was important for me to have a good relationship with her. She was notorious for being hard to get along with; my coworkers were always talking about her latest unbelievably mean comment or new absurd rule. But for me, it seemed like I could do no wrong in her eyes. I always came to work with my uniform pressed, my face shaved, on time, with a good attitude.

I think part of hiding my drug use and illegal activities made me more insistent on a good-looking exterior and willingness to go out of my way not to come across as lazy or guilty. And because I have always been able to get along with anybody, my usually hard-to-get-along-with boss saw me as one of the hard workers. I remember, one day, she told me that most of my coworkers could never look as good as I do in my uniform mostly because of their obese bodies. This was the type of personality she had. As long as I remembered to never complain and to smile when I wanted to frown, I was good to go.

I was made supply officer on top of my other duties. She had given me my first promotion ever in the field of EMS—not something any other person under her could easily say. I also had met someone. She was an attractive forty-something woman. She and I ended up being good friends and eventually lovers. My marriage was good; I think I was just bored. The aspect of cheating was exciting; but the affair would have consequences.

I had gotten good at predicting drug testing at work and was even able to corner a good reputation within my service, which I am always able to somehow do. I became freer with my drug use. This would also have consequences.

As you can imagine, it was not long before my marriage ended. I could have kept mine intact, but I think I was ready to let it go. I had never really planned on having any lasting relationship. I used one relationship to end the other one. In the end, the fact that I was cheating on my wife gave me the easy out. I decided, around the same time, to further my career by going to paramedic school. I felt I was ready. I had been working in EMS for two years and was ready for more responsibility. Unknowingly this decision would lead me to the most amazing thing a man could ever have—a baby girl.

Our family was so excited about our son moving into his first home. We helped remodel it with new siding, new windows, new flooring, new paint—fun project.

He was phenomenal about keeping it neat and clean. The wedding was beautiful. We sent them on a cruise for their honeymoon. I thought we were approaching a new beginning. And we were ... just not the one I thought.

He cheated on his wife, whom we all loved. But in our family, blood is thickest if you have to come down on a side in that battle, and we all got behind our son. It was painful for us all, but we stood by him.

As his mom, I immediately picked up on his infidelity but could not see the drugs. Thinking back, I believe I thought I raised him to be smarter than that. I did not realize at the time that it was not a choice he made with drugs. My family has chosen success over drugs. But with our son it was not a choice; it appears to be an all-consuming addiction that he has not been able to fight. He could juggle it, but eventually he lost the ability to juggle and succumb to it. Game over. No choice. I had no idea this could happen to one of us.

Seven

I decided pretty early on as an EMT that I wanted to go to paramedic school. As an EMT, I could do basic treatment and transport. If the patient required a more advanced level of care (i.e., cardiac monitor or medications), then the paramedic had to ride in the back with the patient.

Now that I had had a very public divorce, I could concentrate on something else. As paramedic school started, I found myself single and with a good job, and I was going back to school to further my career. Paramedic school was an associate degree program and required a score of core courses before I could begin the actual program, which was thirteen months long. This was something I just knew I would do well at. The excitement of the job is something that I really loved. And science had been one of the only subjects in school that held my attention.

My drug use at this time was beginning to increase. I was living by myself, and since I had no reason to put on my fine exterior, I began to get further out there. At the time, the possibility of failing a drug test was what kept my drug use to only occasional pot, and alcohol was becoming my favorite pastime. I think a large part of me always thought drinking was part of normal living—kind of like apple pie and baseball. There is probably something in that, just not the way I drink. I have never really drunk without getting drunk. If I didn't get drunk on what I had, I would drink more to at least get a buzz.

My core classes for paramedic school seemed to pass in no time. I made all As and Bs, and I don't believe I ever missed a day of class. The difference between high school and college was like night and day for me. I think knowing what I was going to school for made a big difference. I knew that taking these classes and eventually getting accepted into the paramedic program would allow me a better position at the job I was already in. I wanted the respect and knowledge to run my own truck. I had seen guys and worked with guys that did, and it looked like what I wanted. So showing up to class and making the grades seemed to be no problem at all.

Eventually I finished all my core classes and got into the paramedic program. My instructor had been, at one time, a paramedic and a flight nurse. She was widely respected and had a reputation for being very tough but fair.

Once the course finally started, I knew right away this was going to be different from my EMT course. This was twice as hard and seemed to move twice as fast. This was probably the busiest I have ever been in my life. I would have class three days a week, and the classes were eight hours long—long enough to require a lunch break and long enough that the classes seemed like another job. At work, I kept my twenty-four-hour shifts. I worked three twenty-four-hour shifts per week and had class three days a week.

Along with all the classes and work, paramedic school came with a lot of clinical hours. They were in all different areas. For example, there were 120 hours on the ambulance, 80 hours in the emergency room, 60 hours in the operating room, and 30 hours in labor and delivery (L & D). When I was doing my L & D rotation, I met nurse. She was my proctor for L & D and the charge nurse of the department and very attractive. I knew that with any luck, we would be able to come to terms. She had the most amazing smile I had ever seen. She was very informative, and I knew that she was interested in teaching me more than the dos and don'ts of delivering a baby.

I was nervous around her. That is how I knew I was in trouble. At the end of the rotation it was time to get my papers signed and set off for home. As she was signing my book, I got the courage to ask her out for dinner. More to the point, she had mentioned during the day that she was going to try to sell her house and move closer to her family in Arizona. I asked her to dinner not as a date, but to hit on some finer points of L & D, and as a trade I could help her with some ideas on selling her house, as my parents were, at the time, up-and-coming real estate moguls. So I showed up that night for our date riding my new motorcycle, Triumph Speed Triple, a nice bike. She was surprised and had a big smile, and I knew it was over.

After dinner and a trip by my house, which I always kept very clean—grass always mowed and everything always spotless—needless to say, by the end of the date, I felt things went very well. I held off trying to get a kiss and went for a hug instead. I did, however, break the next rule. I called the very next day. I think I already knew we were going to be with each other. I had a feeling that it was my decision whether the two of us would be together. The next day we went for lunch and then to my parents' house to swim. That day she broke a rule and asked me to be her boyfriend.

This was the beginning of what was going to be my second marriage and also the beginning of the end for me. From the outside looking in, it looked quite the opposite. I would go on to get engaged, finish paramedic school with flying colors, begin to purchase more rental properties, and think about having children. Like always before, appearances were one thing, but what was going on inside me—a boy turned man who is never quite satisfied—was quite another.

Again, he was showing an interest in his education without us riding his butt. Apparently, the drugs he was doing must have made him feel like a rocket scientist. I should have been more suspicious when he said he was going for his paramedic license next. I remember being so proud of him. I would never have been able to accept what was going on behind the scenes at the time. My husband and I were still working our jobs. I still had our youngest daughter in college, and she had the travel bug as bad as her parents, so we were paying to send her all over with the travel abroad program at school (South Africa, Europe, Australia) because I do not believe in student loans if you don't absolutely have to use them.

I see I have spoiled my children by protecting them from this world we live in, but I cannot stand to owe anybody anything. So we also helped our son with his school, helped him start to establish a rental business, and just kept moving forward, thinking, Everybody is doing great. Nobody has any debt, and we can still travel.

I think, as a mom, you have to take care of yourself and your husband first. If we are not happy, the children cannot be happy. Looking back, I was juggling my oldest daughter's marriage, my youngest in college, and helping my son get his life on track. I was holding down a full-time job and running my own rental business on the side. If there was a spare moment, I booked an elaborate vacation for my husband and myself. This was so we could remember why we do all the other crap. Then all these years later I ask myself, Was I too busy to see the train derailing? Could I have stopped it? I have three children, and I try to do the same for all three.

This is my answer. One of the three chose to take his life down a different path. I love him the same, but I will never understand his choices—I guess because I am not an addict. There must be some truth to the adage "It takes one to know one." I think that is why AA and Al-Anon are the only real answers.

Eight

At some points in my life, I thought, *Surely it can get no better. Here I am, running my own 911 ambulance in a busy and somewhat violent area of the county. I'm newly married for the second time. I am starting my own rental business (with the help of my parents)*. Before it was over, I would own seven rental properties. You would think that, with all this positive stuff going on, it would be hard to mess it up. Little did I know all of it would slowly but surely come undone.

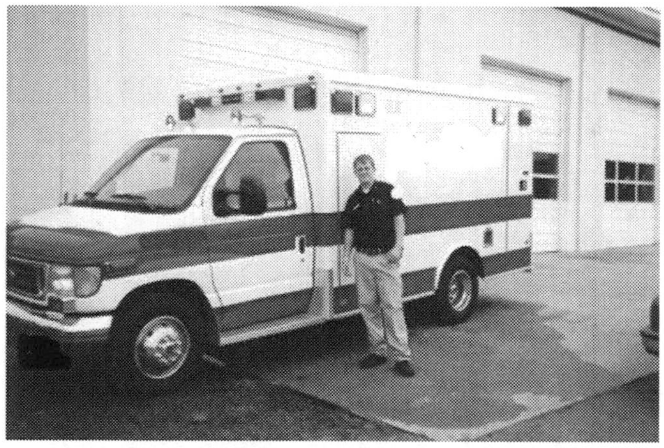

Let me pick up where we left off—done with paramedic school, running my own rental business, talking about have a child. Then my wife decided we needed a bigger home.

But back to the source of my downfall—my drug use and my seemingly endless ability to cover it up, at least until that point. I don't know if it was trying to keep all the balls in the air or just having kept it hidden for so long or having a wife who was seriously on top of my every move. Maybe it was just all of the above and my drug and alcohol use was about to take a large step up.

Bath salts were something I saw in the headlines one day. It piqued my interest because it was synthetic speed, also not detectable in a drug screen. Still having some reasonable caution to throw to the wind, I knew this was something I could purchase at a local head shop for only twenty dollars a gram (a lot cheaper than any other speed).

It very quickly became my drug of choice. I was able to go for days without sleeping; I could work and move at a fast pace. Something else interesting about speed is that I could drink beer until I run out and never get really drunk. I began to do my regular time with the wife during the day, stay up all night on the couch "tweaking" around the house, cleaning and smoking cigarettes. When morning came, all I had to do was more speed and work right on through my twenty-four-hour shift. This was the beginning of the end for me.

My whole life I had been able to maintain a well-groomed exterior with an outgoing personality to mask my consistent and never-ending drug use. Lack of sleep after a few days would take away my easygoing attitude. It was replaced with irritability and unusually slow and rude comments. My outward appearance began to change as well. Sudden and drastic weight loss, dark circles around my eyes from lack of sleep—even to the untrained eye, it was easy to see something was amiss. My parents picked up on it immediately. They expressed their concern to me, which I immediately shut down.

I went on this way through some fairly large events in my life. My wife and I were unable to get pregnant at first, so we began to seek medical help. We became pregnant with my daughter. It was a very nervous and uneasy pregnancy. Never knowing if we were going to lose our baby or if we had some new food to stay away from or if my wife needed to stay off her feet for so many hours of the day. I think you get the picture.

When all was said and done, we had the most beautiful little girl in the world. Still as I write these words, they impact me straight to my core. The only thing in my life that I am truly proud of is that little girl. She is perfect, smart, funny, and looks just like me. I have not seen her for eight months. That is my biggest regret. I think about her every hour; she is usually the first thought I have every day.

Moving on from the birth of our daughter and now looking at a bigger house, I was still doing as well as I could at work and a full seven rental properties were providing extra income each month. Things were moving forward due to my sheer ability to bullshit and maintain and make up different excuses for my weight loss.

The gig was truly up, though, when I was faced with allegations of drug use from my parents, my wife, and even my friends and coworkers. I was fired from my job at the 911 ambulance company around this time. It was right before Christmas. I will never forget the feeling of helplessness. I was devastated. I quickly got another position at the rival ambulance service in town. It was a significant step down in status. I was given an ultimatum from my wife of getting better or getting a divorce.

I will spoil it for you and tell you the divorce eventually happened anyway. But at the time, I conceded and went for a five-day stay at a detox center. After my stay there, my parents worked out a thirty-day stay at a rehab center, which is a sober living community here in town. I also attended ninety Alcoholics Anonymous (AA) and Narcotics Anonymous (NA) meetings in those thirty days. I was separated from my new little girl for the first time and also from my wife. During this time my head became clear, I got my weight back, and my relationships got better. When I got out, I continued with my meetings and working out. My job got back on track, and I quickly shot to the top of the minimal workforce at the second EMS operation. Everything would have been fine if I could have just kept it up

Interesting people do migrate toward my son. He can be good looking, successful, hilarious, and women love him. After his first marriage ended in divorce, his father told him not to get involved seriously for at least two years. "Give yourself time to heal from your last marriage," he said. Obviously children listen to you, and then they do whatever they want to do. This one always has. I knew he would marry the pretty nurse. Again she was much older than he was. She had a sense of humor. We liked her. We accepted her into our family as we do anybody our children love, and our granddaughter may be the only reason we have not lost our minds.

We helped them find a new house close to us, and almost immediately after helping them purchase the home and settle in, the trouble began to surface. My husband and I were still working our full-time jobs and had our real estate licenses and worked our own rental

business on the side. We were planning to retire and have fun traveling and playing with grandchildren. We purchased a small cabin at the lake and a pontoon boat and planned to enjoy family time at the lake.

Our first family gathering at the lake, we were all there, and my son was not so funny. He looked like he had not slept in months, and when I hugged him, he was just bones. I asked him about it and he snapped at me. He spent most of the day alone, fishing, away from his sisters. I was sure something was going on and his wife did not hold back. She told us he was an alcoholic and had been taking pain pills. There was no ignoring how he looked and acted, so, being the family we are, we decided to intervene, confront, and control the situation. We have a granddaughter, and she was reason enough to straighten this crap out. If only it had been that easy.

First of all, being the protective family we are, we thought of all kinds of excuses for his behavior. We blamed the new home, pregnancy complications, the new management of the ambulance company, stress of a premature baby, and the bills associated with all these complications. These things probably contributed to his already existing stressors and had now consumed and transformed our son, in our eyes, overnight.

Nine

The treatment I received at the local detox center was my first my first introduction to AA and NA meetings. I was uneasy about them, not really knowing what to do, or if anything was required. I must have looked like some kind of ghost in the corner with a sheet draped over me. The first night at the detox center, a sober living group came to lead the AA meeting. The leader of the group was a heroin addict out of Atlanta. He began his story—how he'd had to hide and maintain his addiction as it eventually grew out of control and, in the end, into the streets and then jail. I was blown away by the similarities between his story and my own. The two other boys with him and he himself were at healthy weights; they were well dressed and could look me in the eyes. At the time, I could do none of those things.

I wanted what this group had to offer—a better life. They said they were a local facility that was based behind our local jail. As I completed my five days of detox, my parents, always trying their best to help and understand just what was consuming me, were quick to set me up for the thirty-day program. My father picked me up from the detox and drove me straight to the rehab program facility so I could not pull one of my typical bail out moves. Looking back, I didn't know if I would have ever made it if I'd had to go myself.

The thirty-day program consisted of three meetings a day—two at the facility and one night meeting in the community. We all packed into a van and toured a different AA group meeting every night. It was an immersion in AA, "ninety meetings in thirty days" was the catch phrase. I have to tell you that the feeling I had was good. I felt strong mentally and physically. The meetings took some getting used to. Then I started looking forward to being able to hear all kinds of different examples that I could relate to. Actually it was like hearing my life story told several different ways. I knew I had something in common with these people. The fact was they were my people.

My weight shot up as well; I remember the best food ever there. Everything was homemade, and even though they were cooking for thirty to forty people, the food was outstanding. I got into a routine—meetings, yard work, and working out. They had a workout bench and a few other pieces that made a workout routine easy. I went from being a drug-addicted bag of bones to a good healthy weight, and more than that, I felt strong mentally. At the end of the thirty days, we were allowed to communicate with family again. That day to me seemed like a graduation back into my life. I got up early and went to help a local church that was part of our service commitment. Afterward my parents, wife, and little girl came for a reunion.

I moved back home with my wife. Everything seemed to be perfect as I got my job back at the ambulance service and stepped back into my life easily, maybe too easily, I guess. In an addict's world, there is something called rock bottom. I only thought I'd hit mine.

I completely fell apart. I cried. I was angry with my son. I was angry with myself for not seeing it sooner. I demanded my husband stay on him 24/7 until he got him straightened out. A lot of my panic came from my son's wife's own panic. She would call me and tell me things, but I still had a job and owed time and attention to this job for a few more months. I simply could not function. My husband had to do everything. He carried him to detox. He sat there for days trying to get him into a nearby facility. It seems that alcohol and drug abuse is such a large problem that there is a waiting list to get treatment. I searched the Internet until I found a place for him to go for rehab after detox. He agreed to go.

We paid for rehab for six months, but he was ready to leave against policy rules and against our wishes, but his wife needed help with the new baby, and I was ragged trying to work, worry, and help with a newborn. My perfect family had fallen apart. We had no information on how to proceed under these types of situations. My youngest daughter knew I was losing my mind and so was my husband. She had a friend who had experienced this type of problem and suggested we all go to a meeting called Al-Anon. There was a church that hosted the meeting and had a nursery.

We all got in the car one evening and went to our first Al-Anon meeting. We bought books; we kept going; we listened to people tell us stories that made our story both familiar and like a good one in comparison. Our son kept going to AA daily after he left the rehab facility, and we went to Al-Anon once a week. It saved my sanity. It prepared me for the absolute worst that could and would happen. They taught me that this hell I was living was really not of my own making.

Finally, I could believe it, and it did make my family's life almost normal again. A year passed, but I was always skeptical of his behavior. I never trusted him again, although I always loved him and hated the addict he had become.

Ten

Getting back home after my release from the rehab center was amazing and freeing. My wife was happy that I was home, and being around my little girl again made me feel as if everything in my life was getting back to normal. Around the house, everything felt a little weird and my wife was giving me uneasy looks. I felt this was justified given the amount of lying and hiding I had been doing in previous months. I thought to myself that I would surely be able to resolve these mistrusts and get everything smoothed over as I always had done.

Things got better very quickly. In my mind, I was convinced everything was going to be all right. I can't tell you what made me begin to turn back to drugs. I guess if I had not, I would have a lot more and have the freedom I don't have today. As I sit in jail, where I have been sitting for the last six months, I still don't know why I started to seek out another way to get high. What I discovered was another synthetic drug that was, at the time, very popular, called spice, designer marijuana. It was very powerful and did not show up on a drug test. I knew that I could not go back to bath salts since the physical effects were what all my family and friends were looking for. Spice gave me the ability to once again be able to get high and be able to hide it from my family and friends.

This was increasingly important since I was again working at the ambulance service and they were well aware of my recent problems with addiction. Now, looking new and healthy, back at work, it would not be hard to spot me once again falling off and looking strung out as before.

Everything was again "perfect." Everyone was happy with me; I was able to cover up my addictions, hold down a job, and have an amazing little girl. Only thing was I could never regain my wife's trust. At first I expected the odd looks and mistrust, I mean, I got it—honest. As time wore on, it wore me out. Even though I was still using drugs, I felt like I was doing good enough job of hiding it. I was only hurting myself if anybody, right?

This is the mind-set of a selfish, feel-good junky, which I believe is what I was, if I take a brief look back. Pot > Ritalin > Beer> Cocaine > Ecstasy > Acid > Bath Salts > Spice. I could not have been addicted to all of these, could I? Though they were not at the same time, the point is I have always, since the summer before high school, had a drug of choice. We have not got to the drugs that ended me up incarcerated: Heroin and methamphetamines.

Let's slow down and get back to where we left off. Happy, well groomed, on top of the world, all while hiding my drug of the month, spice. As I said, my wife and I were increasingly unhappy, looking back I don't know if we could have ever been happy. I have always been very good at around-the-house stuff, washing clothes, doing dishes, vacuuming, and yard work. She never had to ask me to do any of these things. I'm not trying to convince you or sway you to my side. The truth is there is no side to be on. I was still using drugs, in one form or fashion, and still hiding the whole truth, just like I always had. I think once I broke that trust with my wife, it was broken, and even though she loved me, I don't think she could ever trust me again. We drifted further and further apart. We stopped sleeping in the same bed. Our daughter was most likely the reason we made it as far as we did. This was painful—a hurt I was not used to, I had never really come across anything I could not fix, especially anything involving a female. It only made me more angry and frustrated.

I began to excel in my drug use, mixing once again. I started to drink more and smoke more spice. I did long for a different satisfaction. I had burned so many bridges at this point, I did not have many friends. The ones I did have remembered the strung out me from days of old, and I had enough reminders of that at home.

Work seemed to be going well, everybody was full of compliments on how well I looked with a reasonable amount of weight put back on. It felt good to have the respect of my peers again.

The company I worked for seemed to always have people coming and going. Like I said, was doing well in all aspects of my job. Everything felt routine, and one day I met a new girl. Of course the first thing I noticed was that she was beautiful. The second thing I noticed was the way she carried herself. She was polite, but she did not flirt with me the way other girls did. My wife and I were on a downhill slide. The new girl was funny and polite but did not give me the satisfaction of letting me know she was interested in me. This drove me crazy.

I made sure that I saw her every time I could. I tried so hard to act uninterested in her. Finally I broke down and told her she needed my number, as I was nervous to ask her for hers. She immediately took my number and texted me hers. I did not call for a few days, a few long days.

She is the only female I could never win with; I loved it. She has become one of the most dependable people I have had in my life. To this day, she has never turned her back on me. I had finally met my match. I still hope to make her my wife as I write these words.

I knew from being around his house that his wife felt like I felt. I would never take sides against my son, but it had nothing to do with taking sides. We were all in survival mode, making sure that his child did not suffer as a result of his bizarre behavior. I had seen the drug monster, I knew what to look for now. I could spot a person on bath salts or a meth head when I saw him, because I learned.

In my son's mind, he was normal again after his detox and rehab stint, so the rest of us should have just returned to normal.

Wrong. After the hell he put me through, I will never be the same again. None of us will. My heart was broken, my trust was shattered, and while I can forgive him and always love him, I will never forget.

Eleven

Toxic was the word around my house. It seemed that if I was not arguing with my wife, I was waiting to argue with her. I started to spend less and less time there. I started to spend a lot of time at our local park, playing disc golf or my favorite sport, soccer. Both gave me time and a place to smoke my spice. Several parks around town offer both at the same facility. A particular favorite of mine was across the river in South Carolina. It has one of the best disc golf facilities in the southeast.

I left off in the last chapter going on about the new girl in my life. She has been my favorite subject since the day we met. I will go ahead and spoil some of it for you. I still had to lie to her about my drug use. The difference with her was that she never doubted it, not even for a second. I'm not sure what that girl ever saw in me. I am only glad that it was something.

She, at the time, lived with her mother and grandmother on one side of town. My wife, daughter, and I lived in our new home on the other side. It's about a thirty minute ride from one to the other. This was a journey I began to make quite often. She became my official girlfriend. I will never forget that night. I don't want anyone to think that our relationship was birthed from cheating—much like my earlier relationships had been. We actually started by just having long conversations at work and spending a lot of time actually studying for a class she was taking.

She was anything but easy. She and I knew we really liked each other. I am not ashamed to say she was always in the driver seat. This was a first for me. I was always able to persuade women pretty quickly to do what I wanted; after all, my whole life, I had been hiding drug addiction with well-dressed charm. No, it was nothing like that with her. She had no problem saying no. She carried herself well and once even slapped me in the face when it was called for. I loved every bit of that girl—still do.

I did not make it a week trying to hide my relationship with her. The reason I did not try to hide it was because I wanted it to work. I really cared for her. She was not just a fling. We moved in to an apartment together. It was only ten minutes from where we both worked. My wife and I at the time were divorcing. It did not go well for me, but the truth is that I was miserable anyway. I lost my new house to her, custody of my daughter, and got hit with child support—oh, not to mention, half of my rental properties as well.

Still this seemed fine since I was sick and tired of not feeling good enough. I had never felt the type of love I was receiving and the apartment gave me a place to do my drug of choice, which I did not know was about to change.

Her work was on a different schedule than mine. This once again gave me time to do what I needed to do. I was still spending the majority of the time at the park playing soccer and disk golf. I was hanging out with the friend I'd met in the rehab center. He and I shared similar interests in outdoor activities as well as the ability to get high without consequences.

I used my extra time with him to push the limits of how often and just how high we could get off this synthetic pot. It turns out the answers were pretty often and pretty high. Much like any addict, the ceiling was not high enough, so we began to roll around the idea of different ventures and the idea of trying drugs we had not tried yet.

One thing that kept coming up was the needle. I was told that my love for speed would never be fully realized until I introduced it into my body directly. Of course, I mean introducing it directly into a vein. My first experience was with an old favorite—cocaine. We fooled around with the procedure. The fact that I worked with needles on a daily basis made the experience that much less scary.

It lived up to the hype. I was blown away with the intensity and speed that I felt high. I knew I liked it, and it also opened the door to try what I feel ultimately opened the door to this jail cell—heroin.

Divorce was inevitable and understandable.

As usual, my son moved on to another new woman. He was charming and good-looking. The fact that he was dating someone else was not surprising. After fourteen years of drug and alcohol use, he was at about the same age emotionally and mentally as he had been for some time. He felt then, as he feels now, like she was the only one who stood by him and never let him down.

I will admit that I am offended by that thought and this is why. As our family has gone through this period of time, watching this train as it derails, we have always carried him food, bought gas for his car, allowed him to sleep in empty rental properties, gone to see him in jail, and tried to help out his ex-wife and our grandchild in his absence.

We did stop giving him money, and he took exception to that. I know now that the drug addict in him was where that was coming from. I could not sleep if I could not be sure he had food and a place to sleep, etc. But, if we had continued giving him money, he would have died. Again, when he started wearing long sleeve shirts in the summer, I should have known he was covering up needle tracks. I probably should have guessed he would eventually steal to get the money we would no longer give him.

He did everything I learned he would do at those Al-Anon meetings. I feel like I should go back to those meetings and talk to newcomers so they could have the education I received. It saved my sanity. It also stopped me from giving him enough money to kill himself. He had lost nearly eighty pounds and was near renal failure when he was finally arrested. Thanks to jail, he has been sober for six months and is gaining weight. I feel guilty about him going to jail and blame myself for cutting him off, but it saved his life. He has a long way to go in the legal system and, I hope, in regaining his life.

But slowly some of his personality and even humor have made it back to him—even in jail. The jail commissary offers Halloween baskets that friends and family can purchase for inmates. We purchased one for our son because it has always been one of our favorite holidays. It contained a variety of candy. Our son stood at his cell door and passed out candy to others in his cell block, commenting to each how they had the most realistic prisoner costume. And in a recent teleconference-type visit (a TV screen and phone in both the visitor center and the cell block) he had an inmate of a different race pick up on his end, look straight in the camera, and say, "Hi, Mom," to me. I heard my son and others laughing in the background. (Like I said, one laugh at a time.)

He has also mellowed. When he first went to jail, he said he was "drug-fueled angry" and became involved in fights. He says he learned that "fighting was not his thing" and that he promptly got his "ass beat" at each occurrence. Since then, he has become a model inmate, trusted with additional duties such as cleaning the cellblock area every evening.

And he was shocked the other day when he was kited by another inmate and accused of having a knife. The guards from a different unit and team did a shake down and found absolutely nothing. The guards asked him why he thought he might have been kited. His sense of humor got the best of him, and he said, "We eat with only plastic spoons, and I have not had any steak yet, so I have no reason for a knife." They were only slightly amused and pressed for an answer. He told them he was the houseman, and as such, got extra food for his cleaning efforts. The guards smiled, laughed, and said someone wants your tray.

He is now up for promotion to hall man, as the inmate holding that job is leaving for another facility, and more freedom within the system. Funny how the cycle of things goes on in jail as it does on what we call the outside.

Twelve

With my drug habit now fully involved, I pressed on, with more and more difficulty, I might add. Heroin had become my drug of choice. It was unlike any other drug I had ever experienced. What was different about this drug was the way I felt when I did not have it. I had never experienced actually feeling ill if I did not have a drug. It's hard to explain the feeling; pain, depression, anxiety would be a good start. These feelings were followed by vomiting and diarrhea, which was followed by dehydration from the vomiting and diarrhea. After a while, I was unable to get up off the floor. This was a terrible way to spend a couple of days. I cannot tell you how many times I wanted to stop with the heroin. But throughout the course of going through the withdrawals, I would break down and go spend the twenty, forty, sixty dollars to make it stop.

I started to spend the profit money from the rental properties I had left to get dope. I went on this way for quite some time. All the relationships in my life suffered. My parents knew something was wrong; my coworkers began to suspect something was going on; my relationship with my girlfriend was not even a year old, but already I was scared I would lose her because of all the lies. She was smarter and tougher than the girlfriends I was used to.

Eventually I turned to taking to support my habit. I started at first taking from my family. This is something I thought I would never do. I feel very ashamed of having done it. Then there were the alleged crimes I was incarcerated for—four counts of burglary. In the state of Georgia, residential burglary carries twenty years per count. If you're counting, that's eighty years. I am awaiting trial.

I hope you take something from my life. My story is one of privileged youth wasted on some unending fascination with living a double life. It has turned out to be not much of a life at all. In the end, I was simply using the drug did not even get me high anymore to keep from getting sick. That was the biggest joke of all—what I was out to do, what all the hiding and stealing was for, what my own body would not let me accomplish.

How are things today? I have been locked up for almost six months. It feels like forever. I am located at the local sheriff's detention center, aka the swamp. The truth is that I have not been sentenced. I'm scarred and full of regret for the choices I have made in my life. Days pass slowly, but the weeks seem to pass fast. I miss my little girl very much. I try to convince myself she is not forgetting who or what I am to her.

It's not all bad; I was finally, for the first time since I picked up that first joint in my father's garage, able to get sober. I feel great physically. My mind is now able to recall events in my life that have brought me to this point. The worst part is all the time it took to bring them out and not being able to then do anything about it. After being here for a while, my family chose to come back into my life. I write and talk on the phone with them, including my sisters. I can see no other way that would have been possible. My girlfriend comes to see me once a week, and she accepts phone calls from me. None of this would have been possible had my family continued to provide me with the money that enabled my drug use. My incarceration is the only reason I am not alone, dead, or both.

Please don't allow this to be your child's story. Let his or her rock bottom be higher than mine had to be.

The end.
(Or the new beginning of my life.)

Well my son's mind and body have healed since he's been locked up. He looks great, even in orange. He has always kept a short haircut, so the prison cut still looks like him.

Unfortunately, his family has not healed. I can, however, sleep at night now that I know my son is locked up, being fed and clothed and warm. His present jail cell is safer than most prisons, and he is the "mayor" of his cell block. The many sleepless nights that his father and I have endured have taken their toll. Stress became a way of life that we'd never known. All of our family conversations always led back to his addiction, crimes, and bad choices. While we were consumed by and stressed over him, our girls were getting promoted, moving into new homes, and starting their own families.

Our beautiful granddaughter is flourishing in everything she tackles. We were nearly robbed of the opportunity to enjoy those things. It wasn't until one day, my youngest daughter had called to tell me something wonderful had happened in her life, and I somehow brushed over it and started crying over my "poor son and his problems" again!

She said to me, "Mom, you have other children who have stayed on track, can't you think about that?" She was actually angry at her brother for robbing them of their usual parents. That is the moment I realized that she was right, and I had to change my way of thinking.

I have managed to visit my son in jail twice a month, and his father does the same thing. I babysit my granddaughter a couple times a week and try to equal my time and attention between all my kids. Otherwise, I was all consumed by the drug addict and feeling guilty for allowing him to sit in jail. But in his own words, jail saved his life. I should feel better about that. As a mom, there was no worse feeling on earth, except maybe if he had died. We have all been to counseling and to AA and Al-Anon meetings, and we are all in a transition back to normalcy. The counseling really helped. The Al-Anon meetings were a great education and comfort.

My husband still has to take a couple of anxiety meds on top of his heart pills, but we are back to traveling and enjoying life, and our second grandchild is on the way. If and when our son ever gets out of prison, I will always be skeptical because of who I am and how much my entire family has suffered. However, the god-awful education we all got has certainly prepared us for anything that happens. We know the signs to look for, and we know we can exercise tough love. We know we are strong enough to survive anything now. We also know that you love your children, no matter what they may or may not do next. It's just a given.

I went to court to listen to his charges being read. I knew it would be the only way to hear the truth. As a mother, it is absolutely hard to allow your son to sit in jail for six months (to date) with only the slow wheels of the justice system and a public defender (who actually is a great lawyer who's just overwhelmed with cases just like our son's case).

I cannot tell you how much money and how much pain and guilt this has already cost us, mostly because it is such a substantial amount given the house payments, rental repairs, day care, insurance, rehab, etc. Still I wonder if I were to pay a high-priced criminal trial lawyer $20,000 to $50,000 more, would my son continue to never use drugs again or would he wind up right back in jail. It is hard to believe he would not go right back to drugs, because he always has done just that. Next time he could die from an overdose or on the streets involved in whatever it takes to get that fix. Scary stuff.

What would you do? The best thing would be to never be here in the first place. I'm still not sure how we got here, and I don't know where it will lead.

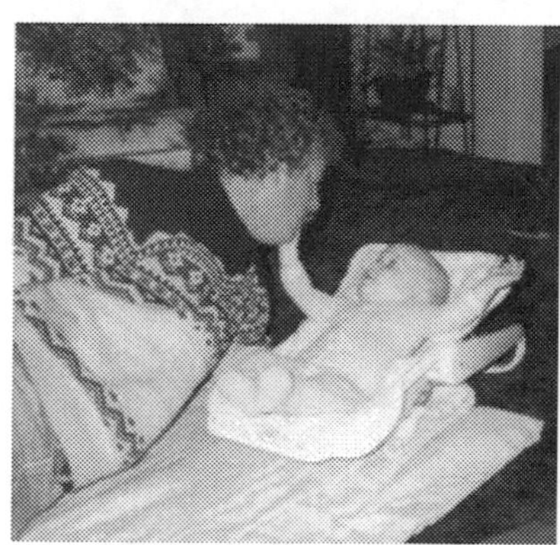

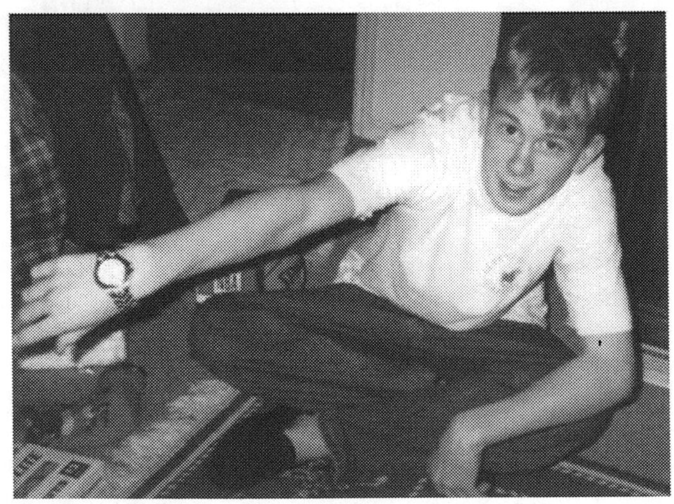

This was our last family event before the train completely derailed.

Epilogue

Miracles Can Happen

The first day of spring this year was March 20. Our son was sentenced to two years of drug court with a suspended sentence of 131 years of prison for residential burglary, theft by taking, receiving stolen property, and auto theft, and the list goes on. It was a long list of nightmares I chose not to hear. Regardless, the judge informed him that no one had ever been accepted into this two-year drug court program with this many crimes and high-dollar restitution. The judge informed him that, should he be late for a drug test or ever be somewhere he was not supposed to be or miss his 9:30 p.m. curfew, he would go to prison and serve a thirty-year life sentence for his drug-related crimes.

When he was released from jail to begin this scary two-year program, I went with his father to pick him up. I saw him sitting on the sidewalk in the sunshine. He was wearing shorts and a T-shirt, the same clothes he was arrested in almost a year ago. It seemed odd that he had missed summer, fall, and winter sitting in a jail cell. He smiled at us, and we hugged for a long time. He seemed like the same kid I had known all my life. I secretly prayed that he was not and had learned a valuable life lesson while being imprisoned as the seasons changed and his daughter was growing into an adorable little person.

I asked him what he wanted to eat for his first meal. We went for chicken fingers. He has always loved chicken fingers. His girlfriend picked him up, and he went home to live with her. That night, he called his ex-wife to ask to talk to his daughter. She told him she loved him and she missed him. She told him she was not three years old anymore. I believe, at that point, he realized what he had truly missed. He was amazed at her vocabulary.

It is my hope that his life will be turned around by the threat of life in prison. Being locked up and estranged from everything and every luxury he was used to may have been the only thing that could turn him around.

I nearly killed my son by enabling him with money and ignoring what was right under my nose. People will tell you to let addicts hit rock bottom and only then will they take responsibility for their actions. Until they are lying in a hell of their own making, and until they have nobody else to blame but themselves, they will not understand the reality of their situation. The past year of hell is what it has taken to get my son back. My first thoughts, when I heard he was being released into drug court, were that I would have to worry about his bad choices each day. I don't. I love him, but I am numb to any more pain he could cause me. The only worry that any of us has now is that he will disappoint his four-year-old daughter, who has managed to remember him and love him during his absence from her life.

A lesson to be learned and understood is that you simply have no power or control over another human being, especially if that human being is an addict. You simply love your children no matter what.